Lighthouse Trivia

10   9   8   7   6   5   4   3

by

NINA COSTOPOULOS

CRANE HILL
PUBLISHERS
Birmingham, Alabama

The answers begin on page 57.

LIGHTHOUSE TRIVIA

1. Which lighthouse was the first built in the United States?

   a. Plymouth Rock Light
   b. Boston Light
   c. Cape Hatteras Lighthouse
   d. Sandy Hook Light

2. Which famous sculpture, built by Frédéric Auguste Bartholdi of France, originally served as a lighthouse?

3. The first documented lighthouse stood in which country?

   a. United States
   b. Ireland
   c. Egypt
   d. England

4. Prior to the advent of lighthouses, what navigational aid guided sailors to safety? References to this type of beacon can be found in *The Iliad* and *The Odyssey*.

5. In which century was the world's first tower-structured lighthouse developed?

   a. A.D. 500
   b. 1600s
   c. 1700s
   d. 1800s

6. The first Civil War battle took place near an Atlantic lighthouse after Maj. Robert Anderson refused to surrender. Which lighthouse was positioned near this battle and the retreat of Fort Sumter's Union troops?

   a. Old Charleston (Morris Island) Lighthouse
   b. Charleston (Sullivan's Island) Lighthouse
   c. Hunting Island Lighthouse
   d. Harbour Town Lighthouse

7. Newport Harbor Light stands at the northern tip of which island?

   a. Mosquito Island
   b. Goat Island
   c. Newport Island
   d. Long Island

8. Which lighthouse off the Massachusetts coast is haunted by a ghost that screams, "Keep away!" in Portuguese?

9. In 1873 the distinctive black-and-white diamond pattern was added to the Cape Lookout Lighthouse. Why did lighthouse officials add the diamond pattern?

   a. To prevent weathering
   b. To use it as a day marker
   c. For aesthetic purposes
   d. In honor of the original keeper

10. The New London Ledge Light, standing in the water between the eastern and western sides of the Thames River, closely resembles what type of structure?

   a. An old church
   b. A spiral tower
   c. A torch
   d. A Victorian mansion

11. In 1835 work was underway on a lighthouse in the Ponce de León Inlet. Which two events prevented its first light from flashing until 1887?

   a. A storm washed away the tower's base.
   b. After the lighthouse suffered damage, Seminoles prevented workmen from restoring the tower before it collapsed.
   c. Funding was retracted in the middle of the project.
   d. An unexplainable fire struck the nearly completed tower.

12. The L.A. Harbor Lighthouse was the first lighthouse in the United States to _____.

    a. Convert to solar power
    b. Serve as a visitors' center
    c. Use a Fresnel lens
    d. Withstand an earthquake

13. What is the main body of a lighthouse called?

    a. The crib
    b. The flying buttress
    c. The superstructure
    d. The screwpile

14. What brought travelers to the West in the 1850s, resulting in a need for a series of lighthouses along western shores?

    a. Immigration from Asian countries
    b. The Gold Rush
    c. Immigration from Mexico
    d. The expansion of the Great West

15. Which lighthouse was the first to operate in the West?

    a. Santa Cruz Lighthouse
    b. Point Sur Lighthouse
    c. Alcatraz Island Lighthouse
    d. Point Vicente Lighthouse

16. How many lighthouses still stand along the Texas coastline?

    a. Twenty-two
    b. Thirty-six
    c. Seven
    d. Forty-two

17. Around which mid-Atlantic lighthouse do wild ponies roam?

    a. Assateague Island Lighthouse
    b. Sandy Hook Lighthouse
    c. Cape May Lighthouse
    d. Fenwick Island Lighthouse

18. Lighthouses have guided mariners through inclement weather for centuries. Hurricanes, also known as tropical cyclones, have destroyed entire towns and some of the most durable lighthouses. Which five coastal states are considered a part of Hurricane Alley?

    a. Florida, Georgia, North Carolina, South Carolina, Virginia
    b. Florida, Alabama, Louisiana, Mississippi, Texas
    c. South Carolina, Georgia, Florida, Alabama, Louisiana
    d. Maryland, Virginia, North Carolina, South Carolina, Georgia

19. Which lighthouse originally stood on "liquid sand" off the Outer Banks?

20. Which of the following is true of the Thomas Point Light in Chesapeake Bay, Maryland?

   a. Although three hurricanes have struck it, the light has remained unscathed.
   b. The only way to see this lighthouse is by boat.
   c. The lighthouse is only active for one month each year.
   d. It was inundated in 1964 after a seven-day storm that swept along the Eastern Seaboard.

21. The Old Port Boca Grande Lighthouse is said to have two ghosts. One is thought to walk the shores just outside the lighthouse, and the other inhabits the keeper's dwelling upstairs. Which two ghosts haunt Old Port Boca Grande?

   a. A little girl and a Spanish princess
   b. A sailor and his wife
   c. The original lighthouse keeper and his daughter
   d. Two brigands who overtook the light house in 1902

22. In the 1720s the French built a fort resembling a castle in what is now western New York. In the early 1780s, British troops placed a beacon in one of the "French Castle's" towers. Which lighthouse site is this?

    a. Old Fort Niagra Lighthouse
    b. Old Sodus Point
    c. Pierhead Lighthouse
    d. Sturgeon Fort Lighthouse

23. Which lighthouse was originally known as New York Lighthouse?

    a. Barnegat Lighthouse
    b. Navesink Lighthouse
    c. Sandy Hook Lighthouse
    d. Absecon Lighthouse

24. Which body of water has been labeled "the most dangerous piece of water in the world"?

    a. Lake Superior
    b. The Gulf of Mexico along the Florida Keys
    c. The Pacific Ocean
    d. Lake Michigan

25. The Victorian-style Sea Girt Lighthouse was the first lighthouse in the United States to be equipped with a _____.

    a. Fresnel lens
    b. Radio beacon
    c. Telephone
    d. Spider lamp

26. What is a spider lamp?

    a. A shallow container of oil with four wicks
    b. A lens projecting light in eight directions
    c. A lamp with a small trap for spiders, which prevents the lens from being dulled
    d. A lamp with a thin protective webbing or net

27. What notable American wrote the poem "Lighthouse Tragedy," describing the death of George Worthylake, the first lighthouse keeper in the United States?

    a. George Washington
    b. Abraham Lincoln
    c. Thomas Paine
    d. Benjamin Franklin

28. What happened to the twelve-hundred-pound brass fog bell from Maine's Eagle Island Light after the lighthouse was automated in 1963?

   a. It is displayed in the Smithsonian Institution.
   b. It sits in the visitors' center on the edge of the island.
   c. It serves as a dinner bell.
   d. The local fire station uses it to alert citizens of hurricanes.

29. Of the lighthouses located in the Great Lakes region, which is the oldest one in continuous service?

   a. Beaver Island Light
   b. Lorain Light
   c. Marblehead Light
   d. No lighthouse of the Great Lakes is active.

30. What makes Nantucket's Brant Point Light unique among New England lighthouses?

   a. It is the shortest of the New England lighthouses.
   b. It is the only lighthouse with three bathrooms.
   c. Its construction budget was higher than that of any other New England lighthouse.
   d. The interior has always been painted green.

31. Sailors report of an area just east of Boston Light where the lighthouse signal is inaudible. What is this area called?

   a. The Silent Harbor
   b. The Ghost Walk
   c. The Quiet Alley
   d. Deadman's Cove

32. The Ponce de León Inlet, which houses the Ponce de León Lighthouse, was originally named after this insect.

    a. Gnat
    b. Horsefly
    c. Sand flea
    d. Mosquito

33. Which lighthouse has no source of electricity or any other source of light but gives light every night?

    a. Old Presque Isle Light Station
    b. Plymouth Lighthouse
    c. Cape Hatteras Lighthouse
    d. Minots Ledge Lighthouse

34. Name the lightweight lens that is shaped like a beehive and refracts a single light with a prism effect.

35. The quaint town of Port Townsend, Washington, home of the Point Wilson Light, was featured in which movie?

   a. *Sleepless in Seattle*
   b. *Message in a Bottle*
   c. *An Officer and a Gentleman*
   d. *Kindergarten Cop*

36. What is the name of the lighthouse and treacherous set of rocks off the coast of Fishers Island on Long Island Sound?

   a. Sandy Hook
   b. Race Rock Reef
   c. Watch Hill
   d. Jagged Rock

37. In 1883 a fierce hurricane swept through Bald Head Island, North Carolina, sinking numerous ships but leaving the recently rebuilt Bald Head Lighthouse unharmed. How many ships were lost in this storm?

   a. Seventy-five
   b. Thirty
   c. Two hundred fifty
   d. One hundred

38. What was the original name of the Selkirk Lighthouse off Lake Ontario?

    a. Salmon River Light Station
    b. Fort Point Light
    c. Cape Meares Lighthouse
    d. Heceta Head Light

39. What is a lightship?

    a. A ship with enough light to navigate an entire fleet
    b. A lamp resembling a ship
    c. A floating lighthouse, resembling a ship
    d. A ship that sinks easily in treacherous waters

40. What caused the series of mysterious fires near Florida's Hillsboro Inlet Lighthouse after it was first lit in 1907?

    a. A ghost
    b. Arson
    c. The second-order lens and sunlight
    d. A short in the electrical system

41. How did Lt. George Gordon Meade, the Union general who defeated Robert E. Lee at the Battle of Gettysburg, have an effect on Florida's lighthouses?

    a. He manned two Florida lighthouses prior to the Civil War.
    b. He designed, built, or worked on six Florida lighthouses.
    c. He rescued several shipwrecked sailors off Florida's coast.
    d. He gave funding for five Florida lighthouses.

42. For whom was the Heceta Head Lighthouse in Florence, Oregon, named?

    a. Don Burnos Heceta
    b. Don Heceta Rodriguez
    c. Eduardo H. Ortiz
    d. Miguel Heceta

43. What noted writer penned the following passage in a work titled "To the Lighthouse?"

"Indeed they were very close to the Lighthouse now. There it loomed up, stark and straight, glaring white and black, and one could see the waves breaking in white splinters like smashed glass against the rocks."

a. Virginia Woolf
b. Herman Melville
c. Walt Whitman
d. Nathaniel Hawthorne

44. What is a "Texas tower?"

a. A lighthouse off the coast of Texas
b. A lighthouse that resembles an oil rig
c. A lighthouse that is both tall and wide
d. A lighthouse resembling early structures in Texas

45. Which lighthouse took only a month to build?

    a. Charleston Light at Morris Island, South Carolina
    b. Santa Cruz Lighthouse at Santa Cruz, California
    c. Drum Point Light at Solomons, Maryland
    d. Halfmoon Reef Light at Port Lavaca, Texas

46. What label did Cape Lookout National Seashore in North Carolina receive after destroying numerous ships that sailed too close to its shoals?

47. What is an Argand lamp?

    a. A lamp with a mirror used to reflect light
    b. The lamp at the front of a ship
    c. An oil-filled lamp with a coiled wick and glass chimney
    d. A lamp generated by an incandescent oil vapor

48. Which Canadian lighthouse marked the entrance to the Esquimalt Harbor and guided mariners in search of the gold fields off the Fraser River in the 1860s? This lighthouse is also the oldest lighthouse on the western coast of Canada.

    a. Memorial Lighthouse
    b. Fisgard Lighthouse
    c. Holland Rock
    d. Peases Island

49. After Portland's Tillamook Rock Lighthouse was purchased in 1980, it became a

    _____.

    a. Bed-and-breakfast
    b. National monument
    c. Cemetery at sea
    d. Restaurant

50. Which lighthouse was built on Lake Erie as a memorial to the U.S. Lightship #82 after it went down during the Big Storm of 1913?

    a. Peggy's Cove
    b. Gibraltar Point
    c. Chesapeake Light
    d. Point Abino

51. President George Washington appointed the first light keeper to which Maine lighthouse?

52. What is significant about Goat Island Light, located near the entrance of Cape Porpoise Harbor in Maine?

    a. It is the most recently built lighthouse in the United States.
    b. It was the last staffed lighthouse in the United States.
    c. It is the only lighthouse still under the supervision of Congress.
    d. It is the country's second oldest lighthouse.

53. An 1852 Fresnel lens has the light strength of seven thousand candles. What is the size of the light bulb inside this Fresnel lens?

a. The size of a Christmas tree light
b. The size of an ordinary sixty-watt bulb
c. The size of a fluorescent light bulb
d. The size of a car headlight

54. Why were lighthouse keepers originally called "wickies"?

a. They were responsible for trimming the lantern wicks.
b. They were responsible for lighting the lamps.
c. They kept watch from a wicker chair.
d. Lighthouse furniture was entirely made of wicker.

55. Which Texas lighthouse did the Army use as an observation tower at Fort San Jacinto during World War II?

a. Bolivar Light
b. Half Moon Reef
c. Sabine Bank
d. Galveston Jetty Light

56. Why is Minots Ledge Light in Cohasset, Massachusetts, often called "Lover's Light"?

    a. Two lovers leaped to their deaths from the top of the tower when their parents forbade their espousal.
    b. The light flashes in a sequence of one/one-two-three-four/one-two-three, which residents interpret as I/LOVE/YOU.
    c. The secluded, rocky ledge provides a quick escape for romantic couples.
    d. The first lighthouse keeper of Minots Ledge was Herbert P. Lover.

57. Which North American lighthouse was the first to have a Fresnel lens installed?

    a. Navesink Light
    b. Beavertail Light
    c. Charleston Light
    d. Cape Ann Light

58. Who used Maine's Marshall Point Light as a studio and living quarters after 1934?

    a. Frank Lloyd Wright
    b. J.D. Salinger
    c. Frank Sinatra
    d. Andrew Wyeth

59. What is an incandescent oil-vapor lamp?

    a. The most powerful oil-lamp used in a lighthouse
    b. A lamp whose light is generated by pressurizing petroleum or kerosene
    c. A lamp lit by oil that glows
    d. The small lamp at the top of the lighthouse tower

60. Local residents rescued the Old Port Boca Grande Lighthouse from falling into which body of water?

    a. Lake Michigan
    b. The Pacific Ocean
    c. The Atlantic Ocean
    d. The Gulf of Mexico

61. Round, cheese box-shaped lighthouses are commonly known as _____ lighthouses.

   a. Screwpile
   b. Revolving
   c. Cylindrical
   d. Spherical

62. Which noted British author wrote, "Anythin' for a quiet life, as the man said when he took the situation at the lighthouse"?

   a. Charlotte Brontë
   b. Henry James
   c. Charles Dickens
   d. James Joyce

63. Which is the tallest lighthouse in North America?

   a. Cape Hatteras Lighthouse
   b. Cape Lookout Lighthouse
   c. Assateague Island Lighthouse
   d. Alcatraz Island Lighthouse

64. How did the citizens of New London, Connecticut, raise money to build the New London Harbor Light?

    a. They started a lottery.
    b. They increased the town's sales tax.
    c. Local organizations hosted fundraisers.
    d. They saved money by building the tower themselves.

65. The Alki Point Light in Seattle sits between a house and _____.

    a. A bank
    b. An apartment building
    c. The Coast Guard's quarters
    d. A smaller lighthouse that no longer functions

66. Visitors to the Plymouth Lighthouse on Gurnet Point near Plymouth, Massachusetts, have seen the ghost of Hannah Thomas keeping watch for her husband's return from war. In which war did John Thomas meet his death?

    a. The Civil War
    b. The Revolutionary War
    c. World War II
    d. Vietnam

67. The Point Lookout Lighthouse near St. Mary's City, Maryland, once illuminated two Civil War sites at night. Which two sites were they?

    a. Chancellorsville and Cold Harbor
    b. Gaines' Mill and Drewry's Bluff
    c. Malvern Hill and Appomattox Court House
    d. Camp Hoffman and Hammond General Hospital

68. Prior to the erection of Ohio's Lorain Lighthouse around 1930, locals took other measures to guide mariners. What device did they use?

a. A bonfire atop a rocky cliff
b. A lantern hooked to a pole
c. A foghorn
d. A torch

69. The Pointe Aux Barques Lighthouse at the tip of Michigan's "thumb" was completed in 1848 but was never tall enough to be effective. Now it towers at eighty-nine feet and is one of the tallest on the Great Lakes. What does its name mean?

a. "Point of the Boats"
b. "Point of the Barge"
c. "Point of Grandeur"
d. "Point of the Baroque"

70. How many towers existed in Florida before it became a state in 1845?

    a. Two
    b. Nine
    c. Sixteen
    d. Zero

71. What is the name of the lighthouse at the mouth of the Columbia River in Washington?

    a. Cape Fear
    b. Columbia River Light
    c. Battery Point
    d. Cape Disappointment

72. What is a beach light?

    a. A lighthouse constructed on the shores of a beach
    b. A lighthouse visible only from the shores of a beach
    c. A group of tall lanterns placed at various points on a beach
    d. The light created by commercial properties on the beach

73. What is a landfall?

    a. The portion of the lighthouse's foundation that erodes over time
    b. An area where waters become dangerously shallow just before shore
    c. The land the mariner first sees when nearing the shore
    d. Sands that shift by the action of sea and air

74. Just after the Civil War, which of these men was imprisoned not far from the Fort Monroe Old Point Comfort Light in Virginia?

    a. Abraham Lincoln
    b. Andrew Jackson
    c. William Tecumseh Sherman
    d. Jefferson Davis

75. What area has been called the "Sandy Knife in the Sea?"

    a. The Florida Keys
    b. The Outer Banks
    c. Washington's coastline
    d. Maine's coastline

76. Why was the first Barnegat Lighthouse, off Long Beach Island, unsuccessful?

    a. It was too short and often mistaken for a vessel's light.
    b. Its wooden structure was not sturdy enough and it eventually collapsed.
    c. It stood too far back on the shoreline.
    d. Its light was not strong enough for ships to see.

77. Which lightship did the United States Navy draft and equip with 20mm guns during World War II?

78. Which is the oldest lighthouse on Canada's Prince Edward Island?

    a. Prim Point Light
    b. Swallowtail Light
    c. The Grand Island East Channel Lighthouse
    d. Grand Manan Island Light

79. Who referred to the land around Whitefish Point Lighthouse as the "land of Gichee Gummee"?

    a. Henry Wadsworth Longfellow
    b. Horace Greeley
    c. Walt Whitman
    d. Abraham Lincoln

80. What is the term for the group of timber beams that form an offshore lighthouse's underwater framework?

    a. Foundation
    b. Capstal
    c. Crib
    d. Crossbracing

81. What do cannon, gongs, reed trumpets, sirens, bells, and whistles have in common?

    a. All have been used as fog signals.
    b. All have been used on ships at some point.
    c. All are common equipment within a lighthouse.
    d. They have nothing in common.

82. Lighthouses in northern regions are particularly vulnerable to ice, even in winter months when navigation shuts down. What is frazil ice?

    a. Ice that has partially melted
    b. Rough, jagged ice
    c. Frozen sea water
    d. Ice below the water's surface

83. How has the National Park Service recently contributed to America's lighthouses?

    a. It is responsible for all of America's lighthouses.
    b. It recently contributed to the preservation of several lighthouses.
    c. It staffs the lighthouses on the West Coast.
    d. It staffs the lighthouses on the East Coast.

84. How did Dr. Abraham Gesner contribute to the modernization of lighthouses in the mid-nineteenth century?

    a. He developed the Fresnel lens.
    b. He developed kerosene.
    c. He helped develop the radio beacon.
    d. He developed the modern fog signal.

85. During the nineteenth century, many builders erected wooden lighthouses. What was the appeal of wood over stone?

    a. Wood was light, cheap, and easily relocated.
    b. Wooden lighthouses took less time to build.
    c. Wood weathered well in salt air.
    d. Wood created less erosion beneath lighthouse foundations.

86. What do Whaleback Light, Franklin Island Light, Wood Island Light, and Cape Elizabeth Light have in common?

    a. They were automated in the early twentieth century.
    b. All are museums.
    c. They were lightships originally.
    d. All are located in Maine.

87. A lighthouse, completed in 1863, marks the west channel through the archipelago on Lake Superior. It is named after a berry that is abundant on the island. Which berry shares its name with this island and lighthouse?

    a. Strawberry
    b. Blueberry
    c. Raspberry
    d. Blackberry

88. What present-day organization is dedicated to encouraging the preservation and restoration of lighthouses and lightships?

89. Which Louisiana lighthouse was hit by a cannonball during the Civil War?

90. Which southern lighthouse looks like a farm silo?

    a. Oak Island Light
    b. Currituck Beach Light
    c. Amelia Island Light
    d. Cape Henry Light

91. What was unusual about the keepers of the Concord Point Light in Havre de Grace, Maryland?

    a. All served the United States in war.
    b. There were never keepers, as the lighthouse has always been automated.
    c. All were from the same family.
    d. They all died within two years at the station.

92. Which stretch of Lake Michigan coastline resembles sawed-off birds' beaks?

    a. Point Aux Becs Scies
    b. Point Aux Barques
    c. Au Sable
    d. Holland Harbor

93. Big Bay Point Lighthouse on Lake Superior, which is now a bed-and-breakfast, reportedly houses a ghost. What has the old keeper's ghost been known to do when guests are not treating his lighthouse properly?

    a. Turn off water while guests are showering
    b. Steal breakfast
    c. Lock the doors when too many guests have arrived
    d. Set off fire alarms when the lighthouse becomes too noisy

94. What fueled the light in lighthouses prior to the introduction of kerosene in the late nineteenth century?

    a. Mineral oils
    b. Viscous oils
    c. Tripoli powder
    d. Solventil

95. Who was the first female lighthouse keeper to receive a congressional gold medal for lifesaving?

    a. Peggy Cove
    b. Emma Lazrus
    c. Maria Younghans
    d. Ida Lewis

96. What do Cape Hatteras and Point Judith lighthouses have in common?

    a. Both are located off the Outer Banks of North Carolina.
    b. They are painted the same black-and-white spiral band pattern.
    c. Both are known as the "Graveyard of the Atlantic."
    d. Both were destroyed by a hurricane in 1815 and later rebuilt.

97. The Fenwick Island Light in Delaware stands next to what boundary line?

    a. The Delaware–New Jersey state line
    b. The Delaware–Maryland state line
    c. The 100th Meridian
    d. The Mason–Dixon Line

98. How do maintenance crews reach offshore lighthouses for service?

    a. Submarines
    b. Speed boats
    c. Divers with tools onsite
    d. Helicopters

99. Which lighthouse off Lake Michigan has a cigar-smoking ghost?

    a. Michigan City Lighthouse
    b. Two Harbors Lighthouse
    c. Outer Island Lighthouse
    d. Seul Choix Point Lighthouse

100. In 1857, when Confederate troops were forced out of Tybee Island, they burned the Tybee Island Lighthouse to prevent the Union from using it. The lighthouse was not fully restored until 1867. Why did it take ten years to get it up and running again?

a. Funds were scarce.
b. An outbreak of cholera slowed work.
c. Several severe storms hit the island, destroying the work underway.
d. An earthquake demolished its base.

101. Tibbett's Point Lighthouse near Cape Vincent, New York, was restored in 1988 by the local historical society. What did the keeper's dwelling become?

a. An American Youth Hostel
b. A bed-and-breakfast
c. A museum
d. A bar

102. Originally known as candlepower, what is the unit of measurement for the intensity of an illuminant now called?

103. What is a typhon?

a. A fog signal, which includes both a horn and a vibrating diaphragm
b. A tropical cyclone
c. An extremely tall, massive wave generated by the tide
d. A layer of rock just below the earth's surface

104. Which lighthouse resembles a candy cane?

a. Assateague Island Light
b. Cape Hatteras Lighthouse
c. Crooked River Light
d. Hunting Island Light

105. Why does Oak Island Light in Caswell Beach, North Carolina, never need painting?

   a. It is made of aluminum.
   b. Its colors were mixed into wet concrete before it was built.
   c. It was built with stone and remains natural.
   d. Its finish resists weathering.

106. The US government originally formed a board that maintained and staffed its lighthouses. When did the board come into existence?

   a. 1801
   b. 1852
   c. 1911
   d. 1922

107. What led the US Coast Guard to take responsibility for all the country's lighthouses in 1939?

    a. A need to maintain the safety of mariners in U.S. waters

    b. An increase in storms at sea

    c. A need for uniform regulations

    d. A need for defense readiness prior to involvement in World War II

108. Which lighthouse is the oldest manmade attraction on the New Jersey coast?

109. What is the optimum position for an onshore lighthouse?

    a. At water's edge

    b. Twenty feet back from the water

    c. Atop a cliff

    d. Isolated from other illuminated structures

110. Which lighthouse has been ranked as one of the most isolated for keepers?

   a. Point Montara Lighthouse
   b. Pigeon Point Lighthouse
   c. Eagle Harbor Lighthouse
   d. Au Sable Point Lighthouse

111. Which writer prompted the appropriation of funds for the first lighthouse at Whitefish Point?

   a. Henry Wadsworth Longfellow
   b. Horace Greeley
   c. Ernest Hemingway
   d. Ralph Waldo Emerson

112. What is a flying buttress?

113. Without the guidance of a lighthouse, many mariners have met their deaths after hitting treacherous shoals. What are shoals?

114. Where was North America's second lighthouse?

    a. Oregon
    b. Florida
    c. Washington
    d. Canada

115. What were "Imperial" lights?

116. Which area has been called "Death's Door," because it claimed hundreds of vessels before lighthouses were built to guide mariners?

117. This island, in the Bay of Fundy, was a favorite of Franklin D. Roosevelt. It is also home to Head Harbour Lighthouse.

    a. Campobello Island at New Brunswick
    b. St. Simons Island in Georgia
    c. St. Paul Island at Cape Breton
    d. Henry Island at Cape Breton

118. Which coastal state has only three surviving but inactive lighthouses?

a. Texas
b. Louisiana
c. Georgia
d. Alabama

119. Which lighthouse do locals refer to as "Two Lights"?

a. Cape Elizabeth Light
b. Pensacola Light
c. Grosse Point Lighthouse
d. Old and New Presque Isle Lighthouses

120. What made the Stratford Point Light's original bell tower toll almost continuously for a total of two hundred seven hours?

a. Hurricane
b. Tropical storm
c. Severe snowstorm
d. Windy conditions

121. According to legend, the ghost of this famous brigand still wanders the area surrounding the Ocracoke Lighthouse. Which marauder roams the shores of Ocracoke Inlet in search of his missing head?

    a. Captain Hook
    b. Jean Lafitte
    c. Gasparilla
    d. Blackbeard

122. Why is the Cape St. George Lighthouse in Florida called the "Leaning Tower of Cape St. George"?

    a. It leans at nearly a 12-degree angle.
    b. It resembles the Leaning Tower of Pisa.
    c. It leans to one side during intense storms.
    d. Its light refracts across the water and shines at a ninety-degree angle.

123. Water vapors in the air occasionally diffuse light from a lighthouse illuminant upward, creating a halo effect. What is this effect called?

124. The Harbour Town Light in Hilton Head, South Carolina, reportedly houses a female ghost seen in a blue dress and heard wailing and sobbing. Why is she crying?

    a. She's mourning her late husband, who never returned from sea.
    b. She's mourning the death of her father.
    c. She's trying to ward off visitors in order to maintain a peaceful light station.
    d. She's mourning her son, who drowned while rescuing a shipwrecked mariner.

125. During the Civil War, Confederates destroyed the Bolivar Point Light tower in Texas and purportedly used the iron to make weapons. What epidemic hindered reconstruction of the tower after the war?

    a. Malaria
    b. Yellow Fever
    c. Scarlet Fever
    d. Influenza

126. Which Florida lighthouse is painted with barber stripes in order to make it visible by day?

    a. St. Augustine Light
    b. Amelia Island Light
    c. Key West Light
    d. Ponce de León Inlet Light

127. The first lighthouse was built during the third century B.C. What was the fuel used for light in this and other early lighthouses?

    a. Viscous oils
    b. Kerosene
    c. Wood
    d. Coal

128. Which lighthouse, built in 1836, has been called "the lighthouse of the presidents?"

129. Passage Island Lighthouse has served mariners passing between Passage Island and Isle Royale since 1882. Prior to its erection, many ships wrecked and sank to the bottom of the icy waters of Lake Superior. What brought mariners to Lake Superior's shores in the mid-1800s?

a. Fur trading
b. The discovery of silver and copper on the shores
c. Fish and game
d. The shore's rugged beauty

130. Seul Choix Lighthouse stands on Lake Michigan's shoreline. Why was this area named Seul Choix (French for "only choice") by early French explorers?

   a. Seul Choix was one of the only safe havens on the Upper Peninsula of Lake Michigan's southern coast.
   b. Seul Choix was the last harbor for more than two hundred miles of coastline.
   c. Seul Choix had the only lighthouse in the region.
   d. Seul Choix's land was especially fertile, and it seemed a logical place to settle.

131. What is a range light?

   a. A light that extends within twenty miles off the coastline
   b. One of two lighthouses or illuminants that indicate safe passage when vertically aligned
   c. A light that has three degrees of intensity
   d. An illuminant invented after the Fresnel lens

132. Why did so many Dutch immigrants settle in the western Michigan town Holland Harbor, home to the Black Lake Lighthouse?

    a. The fertile soil, wet lowlands, and sand dunes reminded them of their homeland.
    b. The town was noted for manufacturing elaborate windmills.
    c. The town had several large goat farms, which were managed by two prominent Dutch families.
    d. The weather was temperate.

133. In March 1880 an argument between the St. Simons Island Lighthouse keeper and his assistant ended tragically when the assistant shot the keeper. Today, ghostly noises can still be heard at the site. What noise have visitors and keepers heard since 1910?

    a. Heavy footsteps
    b. Screams
    c. Loud cries
    d. Moaning

134. What was the name of Blackbeard's ship that sank off the shores of Cape Lookout before the lighthouse was built?

135. What do you call the manmade wall that projects into the sea and protects the harbor or shore from waves?

   a. Large navigational buoy
   b. Landfall
   c. Breakwater
   d. Promontory

136. During the War of 1812, British troops stormed Fort Monroe, Virginia, and used the Old Point Comfort Light as a watchtower. Under whose leadership did the troops successfully storm Fort Monroe?

   a. Gen. Ulysses S. Grant
   b. Gen. George McClellan
   c. Adm. Sir George Cockburn
   d. Gen. Robert E. Lee

137. Many lighthouses have been built in fog-prone areas, as fog can disorient mariners and cause them to steer into hazardous waters. Name the two types of fog.

138. Which Texas lighthouse was built on an army camp used during the Mexican War?

    a. Matagorda Island Light
    b. Halfmoon Reef Light
    c. Boliver Point Light
    d. Point Isabel Light

139. What is a monopole?

140. Legend has it that the ghost of one lighthouse's old keeper moves tools from one room to another, plays checkers on the kitchen counters, and ascends the stairwell from time to time. In which lighthouse does this active apparition reside?

    a. Seguine Island Lighthouse
    b. Minots Ledge Lighthouse
    c. Split Rock Lighthouse
    d. Battery Point Lighthouse

141. Which island marks the northwestern corner of the forty-eight contiguous states and is home to the Cape Flattery Light Station?

142. What prevents public access to the Huron Island Light Station just off the eastern shoreline of the Keweenaw Peninsula?

   a. It has been abandoned for the past twenty years.
   b. Strong winds and currents plague the area.
   c. It is privately owned.
   d. There is no longer a road on which to access the lighthouse.

143. How many of North Carolina's river lighthouses are still standing?

   a. Ten
   b. One
   c. Six
   d. Twenty-two

144. How did many lighthouse keepers begin their careers?

    a. As merchant mariners or sailors
    b. As volunteers in lighthouses
    c. As maintenance workers on lighthouse grounds
    d. In the navy

145. What was used to move supplies at remote lighthouses when a car or a horse was unavailable?

    a. Dog sleds
    b. Tramways
    c. Large backpacks
    d. Trolley cars

146. What sort of ghost haunts the Heceta Head Lighthouse near Florence, Oregon?

    a. A motherly figure
    b. A child
    c. A pirate
    d. A keeper

147. What was the U.S. Lighthouse Service?

148. What is the gallery of a lighthouse?

149. At the start of the twentieth century, lighthouses were home to how many keepers, employees, and their families?

    a. More than two hundred
    b. More than three hundred
    c. More than five hundred
    d. More than five thousand

150. Which American author wrote *Captains Courageous* while living in Annisquam, Massachusetts, home to Annisquam Harbor Light?

    a. Rudyard Kipling
    b. Herman Melville
    c. Ernest Hemingway
    d. Louisa May Alcott

ANSWERS

1. (b) Boston Light was built in 1716 on Little Brewster Island. Tallow candles were first used to light it; an oil lamp later replaced the candles. Destroyed by the British during the American Revolution, Boston Light was rebuilt in 1783 and still stands today.

2. The Statue of Liberty. Bartholdi named the lighthouse "Liberty Enlightening the World." But because it cost an excessive ten thousand dollars a year to operate, the statue was no longer used as a navigational aid after 1902.

3. (c) The first documented lighthouse stood on the Island of Pharos in the harbor of Alexandria, Egypt. It was completed around 280 B.C. In A.D. 641, when the Arabs seized Alexandria, the lighthouse was damaged and its operation ceased. The lighthouse stood for another eight hundred years until, in the mid-fourteenth century, it fell after a series of earthquakes.

4. Beacon fires, which burned on hilltops, served as navigational tools before lighthouses.

5. (c) The first modern lighthouse, a one hundred twenty-foot wooden tower, was built in Plymouth, England, around 1700 as construction and lighting equipment became more advanced. For the first time, towers were fully exposed to the sea, their lamps aiding mariners in their journeys.

6. (a) After the battle, Confederates demolished Old Charleston Lighthouse in order to make navigation difficult for Union ships.

7. (b) Newport Harbor Light stands on Goat Island, which lies beneath the Newport Bridge in Newport, Rhode Island.

8. In 1851, the young Portuguese assistant keeper drowned while attempting to keep the lamps burning at Minots Ledge Lighthouse. He can still be heard warning sailors from the perilous rocks.

9. (b) The black diamonds point north and south, and the white diamonds point east and west, making this lighthouse a day marker.

10. (d) A Victorian mansion

11. (a&b) A fierce storm washed away the soil at the base of the tower, and hostile Seminoles prevented the restoration of the original structure before it collapsed.

12. (a) Although the L.A. Harbor Lighthouse was the first to convert to solar power, there was not enough direct sunlight to power its beacon, and the plan was abandoned.

13. (c) The superstructure

14. (b) The Gold Rush

15. (c) Alcatraz Island Lighthouse

16. (c) Seven lighthouses exist, but only five are active. There were eight lighthouses on the Texas shores until May 2, 2000, when a severe thunderstorm destroyed the Galveston Jetty Light.

17. (a) Assateague Island Lighthouse in Chincoteague on the eastern shores of Virginia has wild ponies roaming its surrounding land. Most likely the ponies are descendants of Spanish horses brought to shore from wrecked galleons.

18. (b) Florida, Alabama, Louisiana, Mississippi, Texas

19. The sands at Cape Hatteras are nearly as fluid as the ocean waters that lick the shores where the light once stood. In 1998, the lighthouse doors were closed to the public, and the lighthouse was moved 2900 feet to a more solid foundation. Cape Hatteras Lighthouse reopened to the public in 2000.

20. (b) The original Thomas Point Light offered little relief to sailors in fog and stormy weather. In 1875, the lighthouse was rebuilt offshore, just over the shoals, where it would be most useful.

21. (a) A little girl can be heard bouncing her ball in the keeper's dwelling upstairs. On the beach in front of the lighthouse roams the Spanish Princess Josepha, who lost her head to a pirate.

22. (a) Old Fort Niagra Lighthouse just north of Niagra Falls in Youngstown. In the 1820s, after British troops placed the beacon in the tower, U.S. officials tore down the old tower and built a wooden tower atop Fort Niagra. This served as the light station until the completion of the existing tower in the 1870s.

23. (c) Sandy Hook was originally known as New York Lighthouse. New York entrepreneurs built Sandy Hook to mark safe passage into the New York port from New Jersey.

24. (a) Lake Superior earned its reputation from powerful storms that arise quickly, endangering unsuspecting sailors. In November 1905, one violent storm damaged or destroyed an estimated thirty ships.

25. (b) A radio beacon allowed mariners to pin-
point their locations in intense fog and
stormy weather.

26. (a) The spider lamp was one of the most
common light sources in late eighteenth-
century lighthouses. Although its caustic
fumes irritated the eyes of lighthouse keepers, this lamp was used until about 1812,
when the parabolic reflector and other,
more sophisticated lamps began to appear.

27. (d) In 1718, George Worthylake and his
family drowned when their boat, destined
for their Boston Light home, capsized. At
age twelve, Benjamin Franklin wrote a
poem about the disaster.

28. (c) A fisherman found the fog bell after it
fell into the ocean and sold it to Eliot
Porter, a nature photographer. Porter uses it
as a dinner bell.

29. (c) Marblehead Light in Bay Point, Ohio,
has guided ships on Lake Erie since 1821.
Its fourth-order Fresnel lens flashes a green
light.

30. (a) Only twenty-six feet tall, this compact wooden tower is the second oldest lighthouse in North America.

31. (b) The Ghost Walk is a haunted region, according to New England folklore. The signal from Boston Light cannot be heard there.

32. (d) It was originally named Mosquito Inlet.

33. (a) Old Presque Isle Light Station is listed by the U.S. Coast Guard as having an "unidentified" light. Locals claim it's the light keeper's ghost maintaining the glow.

34. The Fresnel lens was invented about 1820 by Frenchman Augustin Fresnel. This lamp was far more powerful than others but was not used in the United States lighthouse system until 1838.

35. (c) *An Officer and a Gentleman*

36. (b) At Race Rock Lighthouse/Race Rock Reef, eight ships were lost between 1829 and 1837.

37. (d) One hundred ships were lost, but the new lighthouse stood steadfast.

38. (a) Salmon River Light Station

39. (c) At one time, lightships served as floating lighthouses in places where it was too expensive or impractical to build land towers and where deep waters prevented offshore structures.

40. (c) Investigators found that sunlight, concentrated with the light from the lens, was causing brush fires. A shield eventually was added in the lantern room to resolve the problem.

41. (b) Meade designed, built, or worked on six of Florida's lighthouses in the 1850s: Sand Key, Carysfort Reef, Sombrero Key, Jupiter Inlet, Cedar Key, and the Cape Florida renovation.

42. (a) Don Burnos Heceta, the Portuguese explorer who left Mexico to explore the northwest coast

43. (a) Virginia Woolf

44. (b) An offshore, pile-foundation lighthouse resembling an oil rig

45. (c) Drum Point Light was built in one month in 1883 for five thousand dollars. The lighthouse has been inactive since 1962.

46. The shore is referred to as the "Horrible Headland." Cape Lookout Light has warned sailors since 1812 of the treacherous hidden shoals just off the headland.

47. (c) An oil-filled lamp with a coiled wick and glass chimney, invented by Aimé Argand

48. (b) Fisgard Lighthouse, located near Victoria, British Columbia, is now open year-round as a national historic site. Seabirds, seals, sea lions, and spectacular tidal pools can be seen there.

49. (c) The Tillamook Rock Lighthouse became a cemetery (columbarium) at sea in order to create funds to support the lighthouse.

50. (d) Point Abino was completed in 1917 as a memorial to the lost lightship. The Big Storm of 1913 also claimed twelve ships and two hundred thirty-five lives.

51. Portland Head, first lit on January 10, 1791, is one of the most photographed lighthouses in the United States because of its history and beauty. Washington appointed its first keeper.

52. (b) Automated in 1990, Goat Island Light was the country's last manned lighthouse. It also served as a guard station for former President George Bush's summer home.

53. (a) The 1852 Fresnel lens has a light the size of a Christmas tree bulb. Its intense brightness is a result of refraction through beehive-shaped prisms.

54. (a) Lighthouse keepers were called "wickies" because they trimmed the wicks of the lanterns and polished the glass.

55. (a) Bolivar Light was used as an observation tower during World War II. After the war, the lighthouse was of little use to the military and was auctioned off as real estate. The buyer, E.V. Boyd, converted the lighthouse into a summer vacation retreat.

56. (b) The light flashes in a sequence of one/one-two-three-four/one-two-three, which residents interpret as I/LOVE/YOU.

57. (a) In 1838 the twin towers of Navesink Light in Highlands, New Jersey, were fitted with Fresnel lenses.

58. (d) Andrew and Jamie Wyeth used the lighthouse after it was decommissioned in 1934. Originally constructed in 1832 and rebuilt in 1858, the thirty-foot tower, which houses a museum, is open to the public.

59. (b) A lamp whose light is generated by pressurizing petroleum or kerosene, mixing it with air, and burning it under an incandescent mantle.

60. (d) The Gulf of Mexico

61. (a) Screwpile

62. (c) Charles Dickens

63. (a) Cape Hatteras, located on the Outer Banks

64. (a) A lottery and a shipping tax paid for the building of the New London lighthouse, which was finished in 1760.

65. (b) The lighthouse sits between a house and a low-rise apartment building.

66. (b) Hannah Thomas filled in for her husband as keeper while he fought in the Revolutionary War. Unfortunately, John Thomas never returned, so Hannah has been keeping watch ever since.

67. (d) Camp Hoffman was a prisoner-of-war camp for Confederate soldiers, and Hammond General Hospital was built to treat wounded Union soldiers.

68. (b) A lantern hooked to a pole was the original navigational device. A tower with lard-burning lamps was built at the end of the pier in the late 1830s.

69. (a) The name means "Point of Little Boats," presumably referring to the canoes that brought fur traders to the area in eighteenth and nineteenth centuries.

70. (c) Sixteen towers had been built in thirteen light stations.

71. (d) Cape Disappointment was named in 1778 by John Meares, a fur trader in search of a river. When he decided there was no such river, he named the area Cape Disappointment. Although located in Washington, this lighthouse serves mariners on Oregon waters.

72. (a) A lighthouse constructed on the shores of a beach

73. (c) The land the mariner first sees when nearing shore

74. (d) Jefferson Davis

75. (a) The sandy islands known as the Florida Keys were extremely threatening navigational obstacles. The rough shoals have taken innumerable ships and thousands of lives.

76. (a) The original forty-foot Barnegat Lighthouse was often mistaken for another ship, sending mariners directly into the dangerous coastline of Sandy Hook. The existing structure, completed in 1859, stands one hundred sixty-five feet tall.

77. Lightship Chesapeake in Baltimore was used to patrol the harbor when German U-boats threatened the East Coast.

78. (a) Prim Point Light has illuminated Hillsborough Bay since 1846.

79. (a) Henry Wadsworth Longfellow included the nickname in "The Song of Hiawatha." Before the white man ever came to Whitefish Point, the Chippewa convened to fish for salmon, pike, and trout.

80. (c) A crib, also known as a crib dam, serves as supportive framework in offshore lighthouses.

81. (a) All have been used as fog signals, audible signals intended to keep mariners from getting disoriented when visibility is low.

82. (c) Frozen sea water

83. (b) Although the U.S. Coast Guard is currently responsible for America's lighthouses, the National Park Service has recently contributed to the preservation of thirty of the most beautiful and prominent lighthouses.

84. (b) Kerosene, developed by Gesner, replaced whale and sea oil as fuel for lanterns.

85. (a) Wood was cheaper and could be relocated if erosion threatened. Unfortunately, fires often destroyed wooden lighthouses.

86. (d) Whaleback Light, Franklin Island Light, Wood Island Light, and Cape Elizabeth Light are among the sixty-six lighthouses that grace the shores of Maine.

87. (c) Raspberry Island Lighthouse marks the west channel of Lake Superior. Wild raspberries grew rampant on this island and were sold in town by the lighthouse keepers.

88. Founded in 1994 and originally known as The New England Lighthouse Foundation, The American Lighthouse Foundation works to preserve lighthouses, lightships, and lifesaving artifacts.

89. In 1862, Union troops entered Sabine Lake and destroyed Fort Sabine. A cannon ball hit Sabine Pass Lighthouse, cracking a lens. Lighthouse keeper Benjamin Granger glued the lens back together.

90. (a) Oak Island Light in Caswell Beach, North Carolina, was built in the late 1950s and resembles a grain silo.

91. (c) All were members of a single family. The O'Niels served at the station until the 1920s, when the lighthouse became automated.

92. (a) Point Aux Becs Scies was originally named by a French explorer; it was later renamed Point Betsie by English-speaking settlers. Home to the Point Betsie Lighthouse, this area marks the passage where northbound travelers must turn their vessels east in order to enter the Manitou Passage safely.

93. (a) The old keeper's ghost has been known to turn off water while guests are showering in order to teach a lesson in water conservation.

94. (b) Viscous oils, which left a grimy film on the lenses and walls of lighthouses

95. (d) Ida Lewis was noted for her strength at rowing, her dauntless courage, and for tending her late father's lighthouse at the age of sixteen. She rescued ten people between 1858 and 1869.

96. (c) Both are known as the "Graveyard of the Atlantic" due to the extremely dangerous waters surrounding both of them.

97. (d) The Mason–Dixon Line runs directly through lighthouse property. Mason and Dixon began their survey on Fenwick Island in 1750.

98. (d) Many modern towers have helipads for helicopters to land.

99. (d) Captain James Townshend, who died on August 12, 1910, is thought to have remained in Seul Choix Point Lighthouse. His presence is recognized by the pungent odor of his cigar smoke.

100. (b) An outbreak of cholera slowed work. The restored lighthouse towered one hundred fifty feet above sea level and was equipped with a Fresnel lens that reflected light twenty miles out at sea.

101. (a) The keeper's dwelling now serves as an American Youth Hostel, open to guests May through October.

102. Candela

103. (a) A fog signal that includes both a horn and a vibrating diaphragm

104. (a) Assateague Island Light on Assateague Island, Virginia, is painted in red-and-white stripes like a candy cane without the hook at the top.

105. (b) When the tower was built, its colors were mixed into wet concrete, keeping it from needing new paint.

106. (b) The U.S. Light-House Board was formed in 1852. The board served until 1910.

107. (d) A need for defense readiness prior to World War II

108. Abescon Lighthouse, which was visited by thousands of people in the late nineteenth and early twentieth centuries

109. (c) Light can be obstructed from view when a lighthouse is not appropriately positioned. Cliffs offer an advantage, as they lessen the need for an extremely tall tower.

110. (d) Au Sable Point Lighthouse on Lake Superior is twelve miles from the nearest village. When the connecting path to the village becomes impassable during winter months, keepers use snowshoes, dog sleds, or wait for the next supply ship to arrive.

111. (b) After visiting Lake Superior in 1847, Horace Greeley, publisher of the *New York Tribune,* wrote bitter editorials admonishing Congress for delaying construction of the needed lighthouse. Greeley's articles prompted action, and the first lighthouse was erected in 1849.

112. A supporting buttress or pier that extends downward and outward from a lighthouse structure

113. A submerged rocky platform or sandbank exposed at low tide

114. (d) The first Canadian lighthouse and the second oldest one in North America was built in 1734 on Cape Breton Island. The current Louisbourg Lighthouse was completed in 1924; however, the rubble of the original is still visible at the base.

115. Imperial lights were tall, conical towers built with stone or brick in the 1850s. Built to withstand the ages, these durable towers seemed imperial. Six Imperial Towers were built on Lake Huron.

116. The tip of the knifelike peninsula at the entrance of Green Bay from Lake Michigan has been called The Porte des Morts, or "Death's Door," due to the many lives it claimed before lighthouses were erected.

117. (a) Franklin D. Roosevelt had an affinity for Campobello Island, home to the Head Harbour lighthouse, built in 1829 as a result of the shipbuilding boom in Canada's Atlantic provinces.

118. (d) In Alabama, Mobile Middle Bay, Mobile Point, and Sand Island lighthouses still stand but are inactive.

119. (a) Cape Elizabeth Light in Cape Elizabeth, Maine, uses a second-order Fresnel lens to project an extremely intense light with four million candela.

120. (c) A severe snowstorm. In 1850 the Stratford Point Light received both a bell tower and a fifth-order Fresnel lens. The bell tower was replaced in 1911 by an air siren.

121. (d) Blackbeard used the Ocracoke Inlet as one of his many hideouts. In 1718 British sailors cornered him and took his head.

122. (a) As a result of Hurricane Opal in 1995, the lighthouse leans at nearly a twelve-degree angle.

123. Loom

124. (b) In 1898, when a fierce hurricane hit Hilton Head, lighthouse keeper Adam Fripp was struck by a fatal heart attack at the same moment a gale of wind knocked the glass out of the lanterns. His daughter Caroline, wearing a blue dress, was left to tend the lighthouse and never recovered from the grief of her widowed father's death.

125. (b) A yellow fever epidemic slowed the work. New work crews were brought in from New Orleans, and the lighthouse was finally completed in 1872.

126. (a) St. Augustine Light

127. (c) For centuries, wood served as the primary fuel, followed by coal.

128. Piney Point Lighthouse on the Potomac River has been called the "lighthouse of the presidents" and served as a navigational aid until 1964.

129. (b) When silver and copper were discovered on the shores of Lake Superior, many set sail for the fortune-filled land. However, numerous vessels never made it without lighthouses to guide them.

130. (a) Few safe harbors exist on the Upper Peninsula of Lake Michigan's southern coast. French explorers found a safe haven in this harbor protected by its rocky peninsula. The existing tower was completed in 1895.

131. (b) One of two lighthouses or illuminants that indicate safe passage when vertically aligned

132. (a) The fertile soil, wet lowlands, and sand dunes of this area reminded Dutch settlers of their homeland. In 1847, immigrants built a traditional Dutch town, complete with windmills, parks with tulips, and traditional Dutch homes. The Black Lake Lighthouse safely guides vessels through the channel of Lake Michigan to Lake Macatawa of Holland.

133. (a) The murdered keeper is thought to roam the corridors of St. Simons Island Lighthouse, his footsteps clearly audible.

134. Queen Anne's Revenge

135. (c) Breakwater

136. (c) Adm. Sir George Cockburn

137. Radiation and advection fog. Radiation fog occurs at night when the Earth releases heat from the sun and it cools rapidly in the atmosphere. Advection fog occurs when warm air meets a cold, moist surface.

138. (d) The land on which Point Isabel Light was built in 1852 was used by the troops of Gen. Zachary Taylor during the Mexican War. During the Civil War, both Confederate and Union troops used the lighthouse as an observation post.

139. A pole that supports a lighthouse's illuminant

140. (a) Seguine Island Lighthouse

141. Tatoosh Island

142. (b) The Coast Guard prohibits access to this island due to strong winds and currents.

143. (b) Only one river lighthouse in North Carolina still stands. Except for the Roanoke River Light, they've disappeared.

144. (a) Many keepers started their careers as merchant mariners or sailors before taking over a small lighthouse. As in any career, they eventually moved up the ranks into larger, more important lighthouses with assistants as their aides.

145. (b) Tramways were used to move supplies up steep inclines. The Outer Island Light Station off Lake Superior still has a functioning tramway.

146. (a) A motherly ghost called Rue haunts Heceta Head Lighthouse. She has been reported to be overly concerned about the maintenance of the house and makes extra noise or appears when she doesn't care for what is being done. Apparently, she mourns her lost child and home.

147. The U.S. Lighthouse Service was responsible for presenting cutting-edge navigational technology at exhibits in the late 1800s and early 1900s.

148. A railed walkway surrounding the exterior of the lantern room.

149. (d) At the start of the twentieth century, lighthouses were home to more than five thousand keepers, employees, and their families.

150. (a) Rudyard Kipling. Many believe his book is one of the most outstanding tributes to American sailors ever written.

Also from CRANE HILL PUBLISHERS

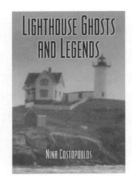

Lighthouse Ghosts
1-57587-092-4

Lighthouse Ghosts and Legends
1-57587-173-4

Lighthouse Families
1-57587-052-5

Pinpoint Guides

	ISBN
California Lighthouses	1-57587-079-7
Eastern Great Lakes Lighthouses	1-57587-080-0
Florida Lighthouses	1-57587-076-2
Mid-Atlantic Lighthouses	1-57587-078-9
South Atlantic Lighthouses	1-57587-077-0
Western Great Lakes Lighthouses	1-57587-081-9
12 x 23½, flat (4 x 9, folded) map/pocket guides	$8.95